Ten Quick Wins
for Writers

How to ignite creativity,
write steadily,
and publish your book!

Jed Jurchenko

www.CoffeeShopConversations.com

© 2019 by Jed Jurchenko.

Printed by KDP,
An Amazon.com Company
Available from Amazon.com

Dedicated to aspiring authors
who love to write and strive
to make the world a better place,
one book at a time.

Also by Jed

131 Conversations That Engage Kids

131 Boredom Busters and Creativity Builders

131 Creative Conversations for Couples

131 Engaging Conversations for Couples

131 Creative Conversations for Families

131 Necessary Conversations before Marriage

131 Conversations for Stepfamily Success

131 Connecting Conversations
for Parents and Teens

Coffee Shop Conversations:
Psychology and the Bible

Coffee Shop Inspirations: Simple Strategies for
Building Dynamic Leadership and
Relationships

Get Free Books!

Thank you for purchasing this book! I would love to send you a free bonus gift.

Transform from discouraged and burned out to an enthusiastic agent of joy who leads at a higher, happier level! *Be Happier Now* is easy to apply and is perfect for parents, stepparents, mentors, pastors, coaches, and friends.

Discover practical strategies for staying energized so you can encourage and refresh others. This easy-to-read book will guide you each step of the way!

Yes, send me *Be Happier Now!*
www.coffeeshopconversations.com/happiness

Contents

Contents

The Secret
to Finishing Your Book

Welcome to *Ten Quick Wins for Writers*! My goal is to help you write consistently, finish your book, and get published. I believe you have a valuable message—one the world needs to hear. However, new authors often struggle to get this message out of their heads and onto paper. Over the past decade, I have discovered ten principles that allow me to publish consistently. In this book, I am thrilled to share them with you. Although the process is never easy, I believe if you apply these strategies, you will complete your book!

First, let me introduce myself and share why I am passionate about helping you transform into a steadfast writer. My name is Jed Jurchenko. I am a husband of an incredible wife and a daddy to four amazing girls. I am also a therapist, psychology professor, and the author of fifteen books.

One of my recent joys was teaching the ideas in this book to my ten-year-old daughter, Brooklyn. Not only did these strategies help her persist, but I watched Brooklyn's face light up as she published her first book. I know these principles work. They worked for me, they worked for my daughter, and they will certainly work for you!

If a book on motivational secrets for writers sounds odd, then let me explain why it is necessary. A frequently quoted article in *The New York Times* suggests that 81 percent of people want to write a book.[1] However, most people who begin writing never finish. In fact, one article suggests the failure rate is as high as 97 percent.[2] Unfortunately, far too many writers are stuck in the same vicious cycle. They start strong, hit a roadblock, and start over. They repeat this cycle until they are utterly exhausted and quit.

I can relate because for years I followed this precise pattern. Fortunately, I discovered the principles I am about to teach you. These ideas not only allowed me to finish my first book but I immediately wrote another and then another. However, before diving in, I want to share my journey with you. I believe my story will increase your confidence, helping you see that you can and will succeed!

Finding Joy in Reading

My passion for writing began with an appetite for reading. As a child, I would bring a stack of children's books to my mom every night, and she would read them to me one by one. On nights my mom was tired, she would skip pages in an attempt to finish our bedtime routine faster. However, I soon knew each story by heart and caught her every time. "Mom, that is not what happens next! Did you skip a page again?" my tiny self would ask in protest.

In college my passion for reading grew. I purchased several speed-reading books because I wanted to consume more content faster. At the height of my speed-reading days, I would buy as many as four books at once, plant myself in a favorite coffee shop, and eagerly read each one. Erasmus said, "When I have a little money, I buy books; and if I have any left, I buy food and clothes." I could relate. As I meandered through my favorite bookstores, the sheer number of books enthralled me, and I wanted to read them all!

Today, as a busy husband and dad, my life looks much different. However, this has not diminished my obsession with books. Instead, it has altered the way I consume them. Because I travel a lot for work, audiobooks are a new best friend. I am especially thrilled when the author himself reads the work. It is amazing to listen to a writer read his or her own masterpiece with all the passion intended. Undoubtedly, this is an exciting time to be alive!

From Reader to Writer

About a decade ago, while thinking about how powerfully books influenced me, I decided I wanted to write too—and so I did. At least this is how it appears to those who do not know me well. But don't be fooled. The process is never that easy.

Recently, an aspiring author interviewed me. He was impressed that I had written fifteen books in four years while working full time and remaining actively involved with my family. Yet there are pieces of the story he missed. When it comes to writing—and many other things in life—I am a turtle. Yes, the word "turtle" sums me up well.

Let me explain. I am not exceptionally smart or talented, and I rarely get off to a strong start. Here are a few examples of my turtleness:

- In school I was not picked first for sports, and in college I occasionally bombed a test.
- When it comes to family life, my first marriage was a disaster. It was a slow-moving train wreck that ended in bankruptcy, moving back in with my parents, and a failed career as a pastor.
- To this day my first books sit quietly on the sales page. No amount of marketing or promotion makes a difference. Although I believe they contain valuable insights, they remain hidden treasures in the self-help world.

So why do I share this with you? After all, this book is about writing with persistence, not my personal baggage. Let me assure you this disastrous side of my life is not something I enjoy telling. Know that I include it for good reason. I share my history—both good and bad, successes and failures—because I want you to see I am a turtle.

Fortunately, I have learned how to use this to my advantage. You see, while a turtle's weakness is its slow start, its strength is its ability to persist. If you asked me what quality a writer needs most to succeed, I would reply that a relentless ability to keep pressing forward is what truly matters. As Aesop drives home in his fable *The Tortoise and the Hare*, slow and steady wins the race.

Although I am a slow starter who learns at an average pace, once I discover a principle that works, I get as much out of it as I can. For me, persistence gets the job done. So, do you remember Aesop's famous race? The hare gets off to a speedy start only to be overtaken by the slow but steady tortoise at the end. The best part is that no matter how many ways this story is told, the tortoise wins every time!

Today I proudly embrace my turtleness. In the pages ahead I will show you principles for doing turtle life well. If you struggle to write or are not as far along in your book as you would like to be, do not fret. You have a hidden superpower, and I am going to help you tap into it!

Embracing Your Turtle Power

Now when I try something new, I expect results that range between failure and mediocrity. This is what turtles do. We are not exceptionally smart or talented, so initially, failure is common. Fortunately, turtles make up for their weakness with unrelenting persistence. In writing, a turtle improves with each new book. After a few years of slow, steady progress, other people look at turtles and use words like "gifted" and "a natural." What they fail to realize is that this so-called natural talent is really the product of hundreds of hours of hard work.

One of the best pieces of turtle wisdom I know is to fail fast, fail often, and fail forward. Turtles learn more from setbacks than from success. As we will see, many renowned writers persisted through extensive delays. Therefore, if you have already racked up some failures, you are in good company.

Failing Forward

Although I published fifteen books in four years, the previous four years looked much different. During this season I made at least fifteen attempts to write a book and failed each time. Then, I heard two powerful words that changed everything. Yes, that's right. All it took was two simple words to dissolve the inner obstacles holding me back. Consequently, if you are discouraged now, do not give up. Your breakthrough might be this easy!

Nevertheless, I should warn you that when you hear the words that led to my breakthrough, you might not be impressed. In fact, every strategy in this book may feel underwhelming. Each idea is easy to learn and only takes a minute to apply. But don't let their simplicity fool you. These principles work!

As a therapist, I understand that change is tough. Most complex strategies are too much for the average turtle to bear. Remember, this book is for turtles and aspiring turtles. The rare outliers who can open their laptops and crank out one bestseller after another don't need this book. These ideas are for slow starters who long to be strong finishers. If this is you, then keep reading. In the pages ahead you will find the secrets for being a turtle who wins the race.

The Gift of Time

One way to view this book is as a gift of time. I am nobody special, and this book is nothing new. I am sure you can learn the bulk of this information somewhere else. I discovered these principles on my writing journey, and you could too. However, by reading this book you will learn them in a matter of hours, while I uncovered them over the course of a decade.

Happily, you do not have to go through graduate school a second time, scour through hundreds of books, or take course after course, as I did. Now these success principles are all in one place. As you can see, reading this book will save you a boatload of time. However, it will not teach you how to perfect your grammar, find a publicist, improve your writing, or build a massive social media following. However, initially, you don't need these things, anyway. In fact, pursuing them may actually hold you back.

Instead, these turtle tactics will help you overcome obstacles, write consistently, and publish your dream book. If you desire, you can use them to publish one book after another until aspiring authors ask you, "How did you get so good at writing?" In today's high-tech world, you do not need to be a genius to write, publish, and sell books. You merely need to be a turtle who puts one word in front of another until your book is complete. In the next chapter we will examine an action plan for getting the most out of these strategies. Then we will dive into the powerful principles that will allow you to tap into your writing superpowers!

Your Relentless Writing Plan

Professional writers are relentless writers. In his masterpiece, *The War of Art*,[3] Steven Pressfield describes the difference between an amateur and a professional. While resistance distracts the amateur, a professional refuses to be detoured. For writers, resistance is anything that detracts from the work. The professional writer is able to stay on task until the job is complete. I aim to help you act like a professional.

This is tricky because a book on writing can become a distraction. For example, resistance may say, "You must finish reading this book before doing the work." It might suggest, "Don't write yet. Work on something smaller and practice these strategies first."

Resistance is cunning and will do anything to keep you from your most important tasks. But do not fall for these lies. You are enough, and you already have everything you need to succeed. The strategies I am about to teach you will help you pull out what is already there. So before diving in, let's put together a plan for avoiding common resistance traps.

It is essential to understand that motivational strategies do not require extensive knowledge to be effective. Learn them fast. Use them often. Then get back to work. Remember, the real value comes from writing.

Writing and Running

Writing is a lot like running. Knowing what to do is easy, but putting that knowledge into practice is tricky. This year I completed my first marathon. On Christmas Day I opened a gift from Jenny, my sweet wife. Inside was an entry to the Twin Cities Marathon. Later Jenny told me the gift was "kind of a joke." She said, "Jed, you talked about running a marathon. I wanted to see if you would actually do it, and I'm impressed!" What Jenny does not know is how close to giving up I came.

During my initial preparation, light training led to little progress. Although I knew almost nothing about running, I soon realized a lack of knowledge was not my problem. Understanding what I needed to do was easy. My job was to put one foot in front of the other for an entire 26.2 miles. Instead, I suffered from a severe lack of action. As the days passed I realized that if I was going to complete the marathon, I needed to get moving.

Although my plan was good, convincing my body to follow it took every bit of ingenuity I could muster. Fortunately, the motivational principles in this book helped me to persist. In fact, all these strategies have multiple applications. They are useful in writing, running, and everyday life.

Training to Execute

Now, let's look at some comparisons between writing and running. Like running, the process of writing a book is also easy to learn. Simply place one word in front of another until the book is complete. Although this may sound easy enough, just wait until you get started. This is when resistance kicks in. Rarely does a lack of knowledge hold writers back. Instead, writers fail because they don't put their knowledge into action.

Battling Resistance

Resistance is sneaky and shows up when we least expect. For example, during most of my marathon, I felt great. Then, only four short miles from the finish line, a major shift occurred. First, my entire body began to ache. Next, a dark cloud descended over my head. I wanted to quit more than I have ever wanted to resign from anything in my life. My head chatter screamed, *Stop now! Who cares what friends and family think? Twenty-two miles is a heck of a lot farther than they ran today.*

Fortunately, I was prepared. In the months leading up to the race, I read numerous biographies by ultramarathon runners—a seemingly superhuman group of men and women whose races often exceed a hundred miles. These runners talked about "the pain cave." In this dark place everything hurts and quitting feels like the best option. At that moment I realized I was in a pain cave. So instead of giving up, I followed their advice. First I took a deep breath. Then I put on upbeat music, cranked up the volume, and with tears in my eyes, I pressed forward.

Pain caves are temporary. I knew that if I persisted I would make it out and maybe even find a new runner's high. In the pain cave I did not need new information. My plan of putting one foot in front of the other remained valid. I only needed to convince my body to follow through. What helped were simple strategies that made persisting easier. As a result, not only did I complete the race, I also achieved my goal of finishing in less than four hours.

Your Writing Action Plan

Your action plan is also simple. Your job is to put one coherent word in front of the next until you finish your book. The next ten chapters are short. This is intentional because, as a writing professional, your primary duty is not to read my book but to complete yours. To get the most out of these strategies, read one chapter a day. When you finish, put this book down and write. Doing this will help you grow your writing habit. Then, when you need a motivational boost, use your favorite ideas to propel yourself forward.

Writing Highs and Lows

Know that highs and lows are natural parts of the writing process. Some days the words will flow, and everything you write will sound like pure genius. On other days you will enter that dreaded pain cave. Yes, writers have pain caves too. A dark cloud will descend upon you, and writing will be more difficult than wading through a pool full of cold, sticky maple syrup. You may even wonder, *Who will ever read this?*

When you feel discouraged, remind yourself that if you keep writing you will exit the pain cave and you will finish your book. In fact, after you publish, you may be surprised at how many people are excited to hear what you have to say. As you dive into the next chapters, remember that you have a valuable message to share.

You are a writer, and you are enough. Because you already have everything you need to write, publish, and sell your books, your task is to keep putting one word in front of the other until your book is complete. Now let's dive into the ten powerful strategies that will help you put your writing plan into action!

Two Words
That Change Everything

Writers write! These two words changed everything. For years I tried to write a book and failed miserably. Then this simple phrase melted my internal barriers and allowed me to finish. Although this wisdom sounds painfully obvious, it is not. At least, it wasn't for me.

I knew my message mattered, and I wanted to share it with others. As a result, I did what many aspiring authors do. I opened my laptop, and I began to write. After getting off to a strong start, a nagging voice in the back of my head would chatter away, saying things like

- "Why are you writing? You don't have a book proposal or an agent. Why don't you stop and learn more about publishing first?";
- "Hey Jed, that's a nice word count, but just think of how much better your book could be if you took the time to learn the art of writing first";

- "Dude, do you remember the time you applied for a job as a teacher's assistant? You weren't hired because you failed the third-grade spelling test twice. Your grammar has not improved since then. You should learn the rules of the English language first"; and
- "Psst, Jed, do you remember the article you read last week? It said publishers offer book deals to people with large social media followings. Why are you writing your book now? Shouldn't you be building your online presence instead?"

I would like to tell you I am making some of these examples up. Unfortunately, they are all true. There was the time

- I stopped writing to study how to put together a book proposal,
- I quit to read a book about the art of writing,
- I paused my book to study spelling and grammar, and
- I convinced myself that building a social media following was more important than writing my book.

Do you see the theme here? For years I missed it. I kept blindly plugging away, starting a book, getting distracted by a menial task, and then giving up. This, my friends, is why most aspiring authors fail. Fortunately, in the spring of 2014, everything changed.

I was on the way to pick up my daughters from school and turned on a podcast. The first thing the speaker said was "If you want to be a writer, then you have to write!" He talked about how the self-publishing industry has changed everything. There are no longer gatekeepers with the absolute power to decide which books are printed and which ones are not. He declared that book proposals, social media followings, and extensive writing knowledge are all unnecessary. Today, if you want to publish, all you must do is write.

I believed him and dove back into writing with a vengeance. *Writers write,* I mentally repeated to myself. *This is so simple, but it also makes perfect sense.* That night I set my alarm for five in the morning. When I awoke I brewed a pot of coffee, opened my laptop, and began my journey.

That was four years ago, and I have not stopped writing since. When Addison, our third daughter, was born, she helped me wake up even earlier. After feeding Addison a bottle, I snuggled her in one arm and balanced my laptop on my knees. Then with my free hand I pecked out the next lines in my book.

Twenty-one months later, when Emmalynn arrived, I repeated this process. Over the past four years I have written entire chapters over my lunch break. I wrote on my smartphone while putting my daughters down for their naps. *Writers write* has become my motto, and it works.

As of today I have written fifteen books, and I have many more on the way. I reach thousands of readers each month, and it all began with those two words. The most important step any author can take is to write. So lay aside doubt and fear. You do not need an agent, a book proposal, a publicist, proper grammar, excellent writing techniques, or a substantial social media audience. Instead, if you want to be a writer, then you must write. Anything beyond this is icing on the cake.

The next time your annoying chatterbox tries to convince you that a menial task is more important than writing, just fire back, "No, I am a writer, and writers write." Then keep plugging away. By doing this you will become a part of the elite few who get their books done. Now it is time to stop reading and get to work!

A Secret for
Writing Better, Faster

If I could travel back in time and give myself one piece of writing advice, it would be "Write shorter books." The first book I published was roughly 55,000 words and 250 pages long. I realize that in the scheme of things this is not a massive book. However, when you are a new author, readers don't know you. Your first book builds credibility. It is a lot like an introduction, and 55,000 words is a long-winded introduction.

From a reader's perspective, 250 pages is a big commitment to make. My advice to my unpublished self would be to turn that 55,000-word volume into a series of three or four shorter books. I would do this for many reasons:

1. Shorter books allow new authors to publish fast. This quick win generates momentum, and momentum is a powerful ally.

2. Short books give readers quick wins too. With so much happening in the world, many readers develop shiny-object syndrome. They get distracted by the next

new thing and leave projects unfinished. Reaching the end of a book feels fantastic. You can help your readers win by turning your masterpiece into a series of digestible bites.

3. A series of shorter books allows you to use reader feedback to give your audience more of what they want. After you publish, readers will tell you what they think. Feedback will come from your book launch team, friends, family, online reviews, or if you choose to include a contact page in the back of your book as I do, through email. You can use this feedback to improve your next book. Personally, reader feedback—both positive and negative—has helped me grow immensely!

4. In my experience, shorter books sell better. I joke that the shorter my book is the better it sells. While this is not always the case, it is often true. All my best-selling books are under 100 pages. Shorter books provide a low-risk entry point for readers. The cost is low and the reader's time commitment is minimal. This makes people more open to buying your book. In fact, if you keep your book short, the worst that can happen is

readers long for more, and this is not a bad problem to have.

I hope that after reading this chapter you give yourself permission to write shorter and publish faster. When you write, don't stress yourself out by trying to include everything you know. You can always write a longer book later. For now your goal is to build momentum and hone your craft.

An idea that helped me is striving to write an inch wide and a mile deep. For example, if you are writing about leadership, instead of writing a 50,000-word book that covers multiple leadership topics, focus on just one area. The parts you leave out will become future books. Readers will appreciate this. As a busy dad I don't have time to learn everything about the subjects I study. Because of this, I search for books that emphasize the areas where I want to grow.

As you can see, brevity is golden. It allows you to build momentum fast. It gives readers a low-cost and low-time-commitment entry point. It helps readers finish your book, which provides them with a quick win too. Finally, brevity allows you to use reader feedback to improve future books. So do not be afraid to write short and to publish fast. Now it is time to get to work!

How to
Want to Write

Since you are a writer, you might as well enjoy the process. I believe writers get their best work done when they are having a blast. This next writing win will help you increase your enthusiasm. Not only will this expand your creativity but it will also help you stay the course when writing is difficult.

Before diving in, I want you to understand why this principle works. According to psychology we are biopsychosocial beings. This means that human beings are a lot like spaghetti. Our biology (physical makeup), psychology (thoughts and emotions), and social relationships all intertwine.

In his masterpiece, *How to Win Friends and Influence People*,[4] Dale Carnegie states that a simple way to feel happier is to smile. Smiling is a biological act that boosts our psychological state. It also sends non-verbal messages to those around us that we are sociable, thus increasing our odds of making new friends. In short, when we act happy, we feel happier and have better social relationships. Now, if you are like me, you might wonder, *Does smiling really make us happier, or is this just pie-in-the-sky fluff?*

Here is why I use this strategy. Cory Reese is one of my ultrarunning heroes. Not only did he run a hundred miles every month for an entire year, Cory also completed the Badwater 135, a 135-mile race beginning at the lowest point in the contiguous United States and ending at the highest. In his book, *Nowhere Near First*,[5] Cory says a simple trick he uses to keep himself going when running becomes difficult is to smile. Now if this strategy is good enough for an ultrarunning maniac like Cory, then I am certainly willing to give it a try.

Because our biology, psychology, and social relationships all intertwine, my goal is to help you become a language cop. I want to assist you in policing your thoughts. Part of this involves eliminating stinking thinking or judgments about writing that sap your drive. Next, we will replace negative self-talk with new thoughts that energize you. Many of these principles have roots in Neural Linguistic Programming (NLP) and Cognitive Behavioral Therapy (CBT). Hence, these ideas have a long history of helping people improve their lives.

As a part of the biopsychosocial human race, what you and I think affects how we feel and how we act. When we say to ourselves, *I have to write,* that thought triggers an emotional response. Our body associates words like "have to," "must," and "should," with drudgery. Consequently, thinking, *I have to write*, makes us more likely to write begrudgingly.

For a quick win, make this powerful mental shift. Instead of thinking, *I have to write,* say, *I want to write!* Or even better yet try, *Today is fantastic because I get to write!* After all, there are many reasons you want to write a book, aren't there?

Perhaps you have a story that will help others avoid a heart-wrenching mistake. Maybe you are teaching strategies that improve people's lives. Possibly, you are writing an imaginative story that allows others to escape from their harsh realities. Whatever your reasons are, your writing matters!

Since you have chosen this writing path, you might as well enjoy every step of the way. Today, commit to making this simple mental pivot and watch your attitude elevate. Instead of telling yourself, *I have to write,* think, *I want to write!* First, change your thoughts. Next, repeat this phrase aloud. Finally, jot the phrase on a sticky note and look at it often. Go over this adage until the words become a part of you.

This is an exciting time to be alive. Anyone can be a writer and get his or her book published. All it takes is deciding to write. Remember, you are a writer. You have chosen this path. You do not *have* to write, you *want* to! Now it is time to get your writing done

.

Three Words
That Grow Persistence

When I began graduate school, our dean admonished us to "trust the process." This simple phrase was his way of asking us to lay aside our fears, apprehensions, and ideas about how things should work and fully engage in the path before us. He repeated the words "Trust the process" a lot that year. As a result, my persistence grew.

For example, when it was time to take classes I did not enjoy, I trusted the process and took them anyway. When I did not understand how an assignment would benefit me in real life, I trusted the process and did the work. Then about halfway through the program, there was an unusually rough day when I felt like giving up. Suddenly our dean's words popped into my mind. It was weird. Although the voice was not audible, the thought had his exact intonation: "Jed, just trust the process. ... Trust the process." I followed this advice, pressed forward, and graduated.

Years later, when I applied this to my writing, it gave me a definite advantage. I believe this axiom will help you persist too. On days writing is hard, remind yourself to trust the process. Then keep typing.

In writing, 90 percent of success comes from showing up. First drafts rarely look pretty. Author Anne Lamott states, "Almost all good writing begins with terrible first efforts." Consequently, your first draft does not need to sound good, it just needs to get done. When I trust the process—by placing one word in front of the next—my book gets finished every time. I am confident this strategy will also work for you.

Today I am excited to present you with the same gift my dean gave me. When writing is tough, mentally repeat to yourself, *Trust the process . . . Just trust the process.* Then lay aside doubts, fears, and thoughts about how things should work. Keep showing up day after day. Type one word after another because this is what writers do. Now it is time for you to trust the process and write!

A Simple Secret
for Staying on Course

When I start a new project, I have a simple strategy that helps me to stay on course: I tell everyone but show no one. In other words, I freely share the fact I am writing a book, but I doggedly refuse to show anyone until the rough draft is complete. This includes refusing to discuss the book's topic and politely declining requests to read initial chapters.

I do this for two reasons. First, sharing my goal creates instant accountability. In *Running Man: A Memoir of Ultra-Endurance,*[6] author Charlie Engle recounts how he transformed from overweight and out of shape into an ultramarathon-running beast by openly sharing his ambitions. After openly posting his intent on social media, Charlie felt like he had to finish. Undoubtedly, accountability is a powerful motivator.

Freely sharing your goal of writing a book will create immediate accountability. Your brain will remind you, "Dude, you have to finish! There are too many people counting on you. Quitting is not an option." The joy of public success and the fear of public failure are powerful motivators. So go ahead and tell everyone you are writing a book. Post it on social media, talk about it often, and wear the title *writer* as a badge of honor.

On the other hand, when friends and family ask what your book is about, resist the urge to share more. I have found that before my initial draft is complete, all feedback turns into resistance. For example, the following types of feedback only hinder progress:

- *Suggestions*—If someone makes a suggestion, I feel like I need to include it, even when it does not fit the flow of the book. This stresses me out and distracts me from new writing.
- *Constructive criticism*—If someone offers constructive criticism, my negative self-

talk tells me my writing is awful. Then I contemplate starting over.

- *Praise*—If a reader offers praise, the next morning it feels like everything I have written up to that point is terrific. When future ideas do not feel up to par, I stress, and my writing slows down.
- *Silence*—If I get no feedback, my head chatter tells me it is because my book is dull and I need to add more excitement. Once again I am detoured from the essential work of completing my rough draft.

As you can see, there is no way to win. Before the initial draft is complete, all feedback leads to resistance. Because of this, my writing motto is "Tell everyone, and show no one."

When a project is especially tough, I ask my friend Erik to hold me accountable for reaching a specific checkpoint before our next chat. Erik then helps me think through how I will get past potential roadblocks. Since I am hyper-driven toward achievement, this usually generates enough pressure that I get the job done.

However, if reporting to a friend is not enough to motivate you, there are ways to turn up the heat. I know of one author who posted on social media, "I need ten people to hold me accountable for completing my rough draft by the end of the month. If I don't finish, I owe you $20. Comment if you want to help."

This writer found accountability partners fast, and he finished his rough draft before the month's end. Rewarding positive actions and creating consequences for negative ones is basic behavioral psychology. Yet these strategies work. If you need an accountability boost, tell everyone you are writing a book, but share your work with no one. After that, increase your motivation by setting up a system of rewards and consequences. Now it is time to write!

Increase Results
with MTO Goals

MTO goals are one of my favorite success strategies. This method of goal setting helped me to complete my first marathon. Today, I use MTO goals to write and publish consistently. So what exactly are MTO goals, and how do they differ from traditional goals?

First, the letters MTO stand for "minimal," "target," and "optimum." These three objectives break a big goal down into manageable bites. They also allow for flexibility, and flexibility makes MTO goals unique. As a working husband and a busy father, my schedule is often erratic. Fortunately, MTO goals allow me to make progress on both my best and worst days.

Now let's examine how MTO goals work. As a writer your primary objective is to write. This is the one thing you absolutely must do. To turn writing into an MTO goal, first create a minimum writing objective. This should be something that is manageable on even an awful day. Imagine waking up with a headache. The children are sick and the plumbing breaks. How much writing can you complete? Surely you can accomplish something, right?

Your minimum objective is the least amount of writing you will do that you will commit to finishing no matter what. You are tougher than you realize. On bad days you may not achieve much, but you can do something. Your minimum goal might be a time goal, like writing for fifteen minutes, or it could be a word-count goal, like writing two hundred words. My suggestion is to pick one format and stick with it throughout the process.

Next, decide on a target objective. This is what you will accomplish on an average day. For many writers one thousand words is the sweet spot. However, be sure to choose a target that is right for you.

Finally, decide on your optimum objective. Ask yourself, "What can I accomplish on an exceptionally productive day?" If you are not sure, then try doubling your target objective. This is what you will get done when you are in the zone. When you have extra time, commit to writing until your optimum objective is complete.

So why do MTO goals work? When I don't feel like writing or when life becomes chaotic, I remind myself that all I must do is reach my minimum objective. Since this goal is small, it is relatively easy to convince myself to start. *After all,* I tell myself, *two hundred words is not a big deal.*

Doing something is always better than doing nothing, and even a writer who only completes two hundred words a day will eventually finish his book. What is interesting is that once I start writing, I often don't want to stop. Sometimes I even find myself in the zone and keep writing until my optimum objective is reached. As you can see, MTO goals are a powerful way to make progress on both good and bad days.

So, what are your MTO goals? First decide on the absolute minimum amount of writing you will do. Remember, it is perfectly acceptable to make this number small. Next decide on a target objective. How much writing will you accomplish on an average day? Finally, create your optimum objective. Be sure to stretch yourself with this one. Use the space below to write your first MTO goal.

My goal is to complete my book, and to accomplish this, I will write every day.

- My minimum writing objective is_____
- My target writing objective is_____
- My optimum writing objective is_____

Now that your MTO goal is in place, it is time to write!

How to
Beat Writer's Block

Nothing is more painful than wanting to write and not being able to get the words out. Writer's block kills dreams faster than anything else I know. Today I am excited to share two strategies I use to overcome the dreaded white screen of death.

The first strategy is to write first and edit later. This approach works because writing is a creative, right-brain process, while revising activates the left-brain. The mind performs best when we use one side of our brain at a time. However, it does not switch back and forth well. Once I separated writing from revising, both processes became more fluid and fun.

To avoid blending the two, I write in distinct stages. In stage one I create my book's outline or mind map. In stage two I write. During this phase only forward progress is allowed. I do not permit myself to make changes until the entire manuscript is complete. This helps me to finish fast and keeps me in the creative writing mode. In stage three I clean up my messy rough draft by revising, revising, and revising some more. I go over each chapter at least ten times before I feel comfortable enough to move on to the editing phase.

When I initially heard about the power of writing first and editing later, I was skeptical. However, once I tested this idea, its effectiveness blew me away. Likewise, I was equally as skeptical about this second strategy. I thought it sounded too magical to work.

I hope that by now you trust me enough to try something new because this is a fun writing trick. In fact, it has gotten me out of many binds. The second tactic for beating writer's block is to sleep on it.

Today, whenever I am stuck, I think about the problem area before falling asleep. I make sure it is the last thing on my mind before drifting off. Sometimes the answer arrives during the night. I wake up at two in the morning with a great idea—so it is essential to keep a pen and paper next to your bed.

However, usually the answer comes in a less dramatic fashion. I simply wake up, brew a pot of coffee, open my laptop, and discover that, unlike the previous day, the words flow. If you are skeptical, please do not think I am suggesting a strange writing voodoo. I don't believe in magic, but I do believe in the extraordinary capabilities of the human mind.

Our brains have the amazing ability to work on problems both actively and subconsciously. By focusing on the stuck point before falling asleep, we put our subconscious mind to work. For me, sleeping on problems worked exceptionally well when I started my blog. Often I spent hours trying to change a color scheme, replace an image, or rearrange the categories, all to no avail. Finally, I would walk away and sleep on the problem. The next day I usually resolved the issue fast, often in as little as ten minutes. It was weird, but it worked every time.

Today I use this simple hack whenever writer's block sets in. So the next time you are stuck, put these powerful strategies to work. First, engage your creativity by writing first and editing later. If you are still stuck, sleep on the problem. The effectiveness of these tools might surprise you. Now it is time to write!

How to
Build Momentum Fast

It was two in the morning, and I was working the overnight shift at a group home. On this particular night I was feeling down. *How can I be a therapist and help other people improve their lives when I make so many mistakes myself?* I wondered. I felt like a failure, and my exhausted brain was doing an outstanding job of convincing me I was not good at anything.

One of my nightly duties involved basic cleaning, and I was off to a slow start. With morning approaching, I figured I'd better get to work. I tied up the overflowing garbage bags, took them to the dumpster, and wiped the trashcans clean. *That looks better*, I thought to myself. *Ok, so I guess I can do something right. And if I can do a good job taking out the trash, then I'm sure I can do an excellent job of sweeping the floors.* I grabbed a broom and got to work.

I guess I'm not too bad at sweeping either. And if I can sweep well, then I am pretty sure I can do a decent job of mopping. With the completion of each new task, I felt my confidence grow. As I continued to clean, I thought back to all the school assignments I had successfully completed. I mentally reminded myself, *Since I got an A in my last class, I can get an A in my next class too.* I continued to search for small wins, and I mentally celebrated the rest of the night. By the time the sun rose, I was energized.

I used this strategy night after night. Whenever I felt inept, I reminded myself that if I could do small tasks well, then I could certainly do big tasks well too. After all, most large jobs are only a series of smaller ones strung together. Soon the *If... Then... Technique* was born.

When students in the college courses I teach struggle with their assignments, I remind them, "If you can write one sentence, then you can write another and another. Once you have three sentences, you've finished your first paragraph. And if you can write one paragraph, then you can write another." I encourage students to break large assignments into a series of small missions and celebrate each victory.

I once heard an athlete define running as placing one foot in front of another. A marathon feels overwhelming when you focus on the miles that remain. Similarly, writing a book is stressful when writers concentrate on the amount of work left. In reality, the size of the book does not matter.

Remember, writing is nothing more than placing one word in front of the other. If you can write one sentence, then you can write another. You can use this process to write a short book or a long one because length only determines how long the project takes. Since you are able to put one sentence in front of the next, we have already established that you are capable of writing a book. After all, even the longest books are written one sentence at a time.

Recently I learned that ultrarunner David Goggins—who many consider the toughest man alive—employs a similar strategy. In his book, *Can't Hurt Me,* David outlines his cookie-jar technique. David keeps a mental cookie jar packed with memories of past successes. During difficult runs he reaches inside and gets a psychological boost. In other words, David looks to past victories to fuel his current endeavors.

The next time you feel discouraged, put this strategy to work. First reach into your cookie jar and pull out an old victory. After meditating on your past success, set a small, achievable goal. This can be as simple as writing one sentence. Then smile or perform a quick victory dance. You have now generated some momentum. Keep this going by writing another sentence fast. Remind yourself that you have overcome obstacles before and you will succeed again.

The *If... Then... Technique* is a powerful momentum builder. In fact, let's use it right now. If you've accomplished your writing goal in the past, then you are capable of reaching your goal again today. Now it is time to get to work!

A Powerful Phrase
for Laser Focus

My wife, Jenny, joined a cosmetics business and was excited about an upcoming training call. Suddenly she blurted out some dreaded words: "Hey, honey, tonight's call is after the children's bedtime. Why don't you join me? You'll learn about what I do, and spending time together will be fun."

There is no way that a seminar on makeup is going to be fun, I thought to myself. As you can imagine, my expectations were low. Nevertheless, out of a desire to support my wife, I agreed. Much to my delight the teaching was transformational.

Instead of focusing on lipstick and mascara, the trainer zeroed in on a powerful success strategy. The speaker proposed that we focus only on outcomes we can control. He suggested taking 100 percent responsibility for our actions and not stressing over the immediate results. A phrase he repeated often was "Do the work, and you will get there when you get there."[7]

During the call consultants asked questions like:

- How many daily calls do I need to make to earn a full-time income?
- How long will it take to reach my goal of becoming a company director?
- How many leads a day do I need to generate to achieve my goal?

These consultants wanted to set big goals. However, these types of goals have at least three problems:

1. Creating complex numbers goals takes a lot of mental energy, and this energy is better spent on getting the work done.
2. It is easy to fall behind because these goals are often unrealistic or have outcomes outside of our direct control.
3. Once we fall behind, resistance kicks in. We think to ourselves, *Since I won't reach my goal this month, I'll stop now and get back on track next month.* Then we quit doing the work.

At first, big goals feel energizing, but once momentum is lost, they are counterproductive. At least, this has been my experience. I avoid this energy sap by zeroing in on actions with controllable outcomes. Then I take 100 percent responsibility for getting those tasks done. I am learning not to worry about how long it takes to reach my goal but, instead, to keep a laser-like focus on doing the right actions. In other words, my attitude is "I'm going to do the work, and I will get there when I get there."

This means not stressing over getting my book published by a specific date, worrying about how many people buy my books, or feeling pressured to get a certain number of reviews. These things are outside of my control. Instead, I start by writing because I can take 100 percent responsibility for this. Then I take 100 percent responsibility for asking others to read my book and for asking people to write a review. Although I cannot control these outcomes, I can take full responsibility for asking.

A good friend once said, "Jed, you might as well ask. People can't say yes if you don't, and the worst they can say is no if you do." Of course, asking still makes me nervous. However, once I act I am usually blown away by how kind, engaging, and responsive people are. Moreover, when the outcomes are not as positive as I would like, I remind myself, "Jed, get back to work. You will get there when you get there." This simple phrase motivates me to press forward every time.

Although this mental pivot is small, it is powerful. Taking the focus off outcomes I cannot control and focusing only on areas where I can take 100 percent responsibility decreases my anxiety and increases my momentum. I would encourage you to do the same. This could mean

- dedicating one hour a day to researching your next book for the next week,
- committing to writing one thousand words a day,
- asking ten people if they will read your book and leave an honest review, or
- asking ten friends to share your book on social media.

Under this model, you are responsible for doing the research, doing the writing, and for making the ask. Then celebrate any positive outcomes regardless of how small or large they are. As you know, life is not fair. So don't fret if other authors progress faster than you. Keep showing up until you achieve your goal.

I found that most projects take twice as long as I expect, and if this happens to you, know this is normal. On the other hand, when I look at the number of books I have published, I am further along than I expected. Perhaps this is why Bill Gates said, "Most people overestimate what they can do in one year and underestimate what they can do in ten years."

The next time your internal chatterbox asks, "How long will it take?" and "Why are other authors further along than I am?" refuse to be detoured. Simply reply, "It doesn't matter; I am doing the work, and I'll get there when I get there." Then tackle your next task with laser-intensity. Now it is time to get to work!

A Powerful
Motivation Metaphor

Writing has been described as puking on paper and smearing the mess around until something beautiful emerges. Others have used the more graphic metaphor of slitting one's wrist and creating a masterpiece out of one's own blood. These vivid descriptions remind me that writing can be messy and painful.

Thomas Mann said, "A writer is someone for whom writing is more difficult than it is for other people." I agree. Many writers struggle with self-doubt, self-loathing, and sometimes just with themselves in general.

Part of the reason is that publishing requires vulnerability. It takes courage to put one's soul on display. Before my first blog post went live, my finger hovered above the keyboard for an entire fifteen minutes. Yes, it took that long to work up the courage to publish. Fortunately, sharing what I write has become easier with practice and the use of one simple strategy.

Before publishing anything, I remind myself, *This is an experiment.* I picture a mad scientist holding a beaker in each hand. He has a big smile on his face and a maniacal laugh. Then I envision myself as a mad scientist too.

Have you ever wondered why mad scientists wear those mischievous smiles? It is because they know that once they start their experiment they will be wiser than they are now. After the beakers mix, there could be a noxious explosion or the scientist might uncover the secret for turning lead into gold. The only way to find out is to perform the experiment.

If the test fails, the scientist learns one more way it does not work and is wiser as a result. When creating the lightbulb, Thomas Edison said, "I have not failed. I've just discovered 10,000 ways that don't work." As tradition has it, Edison's success came on attempt 10,001.

In publishing, I never know what to expect. Sometimes books I pour my heart into receive little attention. On other occasions books written on a whim attain best-seller status. Nowadays I remind myself, *Jed, you do not know what the results will be. So publish your book and find out. Remember, this is an experiment. It is time to complete this one so you can move on to the next one. After all, this is how scientists progress.*

This self-talk helps me to maintain a detached curiosity. My book does not have to live up to my expectations. Rather, my job is to write, publish, gather data, and repeat. All scientists eventually have breakthroughs. If you keep writing and keep learning, you will improve your ability to connect with your audience.

So let go of expectations. Instead, adopt the mad scientist attitude of curiosity and growth. Do this by telling yourself, *This is an experiment.* Then get back to writing. Now it is time for you to get back to your writing experiment!

Redefining Writing Success

Studying success principles has convinced me that those who succeed at their craft have one thing in common. They will not be denied. Successful people are hyper-focused on their mission and press forward until they get the results they want. Successful authors are not always the smartest, most talented, or most skilled. Sometimes they merely outlast everyone else. For example,

- Stephen King received 30 rejection slips before his first book, *Carrie,* was published.[8]
- J. K. Rowling received 12 rejections for *Harry Potter.*[9]
- The Pulitzer Prize classic *Gone with the Wind* received a surprising 38 rejections before finding its publisher.[10]
- Moreover, Jack Canfield and Mark Victor Hansen's wildly successful book, *Chicken Soup for the Soul*, received an astounding 134 rejections before being published.[11]

If you have ever been rejected, then congratulations, you are in good company. Rejection adds you to a long list of authors who ran headfirst into a brick wall, kept going, and succeeded anyway. The best writers do not always have a smooth path to the top, nor do they get things right the first time. What separates a professional from the thousands of other writers with unpublished manuscripts stored on their hard drives is a dogged refusal to resign. Jack Canfield's advice is to "reject rejection. If someone says no, just say NEXT!"[12]

One of my all-time favorite quotes comes from Randy Pausch, co-author of *The Last Lecture*.[10] Randy's book birthed out of a lecture he gave at Carnegie Mellon University in September 2007. Each year the university asks an esteemed professor to give an inspiring speech. The professor's role is to act as if this will be the last lecture he or she gives. Randy's story is unique because shortly after agreeing to the speech he was diagnosed with terminal cancer. For Randy, *The Last Lecture* was actually going to be his last lecture.

In his talk Randy says, "The brick walls are there for a reason. The brick walls are not there to keep us out; the brick walls are there to give us a chance to show how badly we want something. The brick walls are there to stop the people who don't want it badly enough. They are there to stop the other people."[13]

In concluding this book, I want to again encourage you to keep writing. My only fear is that this encouragement will be mistaken as fluff. I have been accused of writing "encouraging fluff" before. Happily, I am learning to wear this as a badge of honor. You see, I believe this criticism comes from those who don't get it.

Sometimes I wonder if people who quit pursuing their dreams are looking for a way out. Perhaps believing that success comes from giftings they lack makes giving up easier to bear. Yet genetic giftings are only small pieces of the puzzle. Success also comes from showing up day after day. This is why I believe motivational speakers and writers provide an invaluable service. We all need encouragers who inspire us to show up.

There are no shortcuts to achieving your writing dreams. As we have seen, all books are written the same way. One word is placed in front of the next until the manuscript is complete. This is true whether you type, dictate, or pay a ghostwriter to transcribe your ideas. Regardless, the process of putting one word after the next cannot be skipped.

Success is rooted in grit. So keep pressing forward. Do not let brick walls stand in your way. When you enter a pain cave and your writing feels worthless, continue to write anyway. Most of all, remember that you are a writer. You have a message to share. Now is the time to get it on paper and present it to the world. I wish you much writing success.

Bonus:
Write Your Book
in a Weekend

Recently, I read an article suggesting that an author can write a book in a weekend. When I first read this, I thought, *That's absurd! Even if someone could finish a book that fast, there is no way it would be any good.*

Just because something can be done does not mean it should be done. A good book inspires change, offers hope, and teaches invaluable skills. It does not sound reasonable to accomplish this in a weekend. However, I have changed my opinion. I now believe it is possible to write a respectable book that fast. But there is a catch.

When I first pictured someone accomplishing this, I imagined them starting from scratch. They would choose their topic, do research, and get the writing done. I have discovered that the process looks much different. Authors who finish a book in a weekend are typically already experts in their field. Perhaps they have given speeches or have written extensively on their blog.

When I set out to write this book, I had no intention of finishing it in two days, but I did. Four things made this possible. First, this book is packed with principles I learned over the course of a decade. I teach these ideas often and use them daily. As a result, the content flowed.

Second, I began with a solid outline in place. This preparation was done earlier, and it allowed me to transition from one chapter to the next with ease. Thus, even though I wrote the book in a weekend, the groundwork was years in the making.

Third, this book is short, which also helped me to finish fast. Of course, longer books will require more time. Finally, although the rough draft was finished fast, I revised it daily over the next three weeks. In the end, nearly a hundred hours of work went into this tiny book.

So is it possible to write a book in a weekend? Yes and no. Technically, it is doable if you are an expert in your field, choose to keep the book short, and spend the following weeks cleaning up the messy rough draft. I share this with you because I want to pull back the curtain and reveal what the process actually looks like.

For me, writing is the fun, creative part. Revising, refining, and editing are where the real work lays. However, do not fret. The same motivational strategies you learned in this book will serve you well during the later phases too.

In short, do not be deceived by anyone who promises a quick and easy approach to writing success. A good book requires effort, and success is typically the product of years of struggle. In *Outliers*, Malcolm Gladwell's masterpiece on the science of elite performance, Gladwell suggests, "You need to have practiced, to have apprenticed, for 10,000 hours before you get good."[14] This 10,000-hour rule certainly applies to writers.

So once again, keep pressing forward. For your next book you may want to choose a topic you already know a lot about and write your book in a weekend too. I genuinely believe your writing future is bright—so bright that you may need to wear shades!

Sincerely, Jed Jurchenko

End Notes

1. Epstein, Joseph, **"Think You Have a Book in You? Think Again,"** The New York Times, September 28, 2002, https://www.nytimes.com/2002/09/28/opinion/think-you-have-a-book-in-you-think-again.html.

2. Zink, Sharon, "97% of Writers Never Finish Their Novels: Here's Why," *Sharon Zink* (blog), May 23, 2017, http://sharonzink.com/writing-tips/97-of-writers-never-finish-their-novels-heres-why/.

3. Pressfield, Steven, *The War of Art*. Black Irish Entertainment LLC, November 11, 2011.

4. Carnegie, Dale, *How to Win Friends and Influence People* (New York: Pocket Books, 1998).

5. Reese, Cory, *Nowhere Near First* (N.p.: CreateSpace, 2016).

6. Engle, Charlie, *Running Man: A Memoir of Ultra-Endurance* (New York: Scribner, 2017).

7. Quoted attributed to Sean Smith. https://pinkcaddiecoach.com/

8. "17 World Famous Authors Who Were Rejected Repeatedly Before Hitting It Big," BrainJet, 2019, https://www.brainjet.com/random/2359010/17-world-famous-authors-who-were-rejected-repeatedly-before-hitting-it-big/.

9. Temple, Emily, "The Most Rejected Books of All Time," Literary Hub, December 22, 2017, https://lithub.com/the-most-rejected-books-of-all-time/

10. Ibid

11. Ibid

12. Ibid

13. Pausch, Randy and Jeffery Zaslow, *The Last Lecture*. (New York: Hachette, 2008).

14. Gladwell, Malcolm, *Outliers*: *The Story of Success*. (New York: Little, Brown and Company, 2008).

Thumbs Up
or Thumbs Down

Thank you for purchasing this book!

I would love to hear from you! Your feedback not only helps me grow as a writer but also helps me to get books into the hands of those who need them most. Online reviews are one of the most significant ways independent authors like me connect with new readers.

If you loved the book, could you please share your experience? Leaving feedback is as easy as answering any of these questions:

- What did you like about the book?

- What is your most valuable takeaway from this book?
- What have you done differently, or what will you do differently because of what you have read?
- To whom would you recommend this book?

Of course, I am looking for honest reviews. So if you have a minute to share your experience, good or bad, please consider leaving a review!

I look forward to hearing from you!

Sincerely, Jed Jurchenko

About the Author

Jed is passionate about helping people live happy, healthy, more connected lives by having better conversations. He is a husband, father of four girls, a psychology professor, therapist, and writer.

Jed graduated from Southern California Seminary with a Master of Divinity and returned to complete a second master's degree in psychology. In his free time Jed enjoys walking on the beach, reading, and spending time with his incredible family.

Continue the Conversation

If you enjoyed this book, I would love it if you would leave a review. Your feedback is an enormous encouragement to me, and it helps books like this one get noticed. It only takes a minute, and every review is much appreciated. Oh, and please feel free to stay in touch too!

Email: jed@coffeeshopconversations.com

Twitter: @jjurchenko

Facebook: Coffee Shop Conversations

Blog: www.CoffeeShopConversations.com

More Books by Jed

This book and other creative conversation starters are available at www.Amazon.com.

Transform your relationship from dull and bland to inspired, passionate, and connected as you grow your insights into your spouse's inner world! Whether you are newly dating or nearing your golden anniversary, these questions are for you! This book will help you share your heart and dive into your partner's inner world.

131 Creative Conversations for Couples

More Books by Jed

These creative conversation starters will inspire your kids to pause their electronics, grow their social skills, and develop lifelong relationships!

This book is for children and tweens who desire to build face-to-face connections and everyone who wants to help their kids connect in an increasingly disconnected world. Get your kids talking with this activity book the entire family will enjoy.

131 Conversations That Engage Kids

72779104R00046

Made in the USA
Columbia, SC
31 August 2019